Things my kids say (in limerick)

AF290907

Pauline Glasson

BookLeaf Publishing

Things my kids say (in limerick) © 2022
Pauline Glasson

All rights reserved.

No part of this publication may be reproduced, stored in a retrieval system, or transmitted, in any form or by any means, electronic, mechanical, photocopying, recording or otherwise, without the prior written permission of the presenters.

Pauline Glasson asserts the moral right to be identified as author of this work.

Presentation by *BookLeaf Publishing*

Web: www.bookleafpub.com

E-mail: info@bookleafpub.com

ISBN: 9789357616928

First edition 2022

*To Max and Alex for your honest musings
about our world. To my wonderful husband
and best friend Greg who shares these
moments.*

The plane

I was sitting in the airport with my son
"Do you know what our next plane will be
mom?"
"A big one?" I said
He titled his head
"Bet it's bigger than the Fokker we flew in on"

Hereditary

2

Our son doesn't like going to school
To my husband I say "he's a mini you"
"Before we identify
The tree he sits by
You both walked into a wall tis true"

Deception

I announce "it's time for a bath"
No sounds come from the correct path
"Mum you can't see me
I'm not near the TV"
"Yes you are! I can do math!"

Discovery

In the car we sat with our lad
Talking of holidays we've had
"Epic we are
to take you so far"
Our son asks "you're not my dad?"

Unease

5

It is just us in the house
You, me and the cat
My son turns to say
Expressionlessly
"And the murderous pineapples"

History

My son is quite the jester
When he asked about ancestors
"Sit here mum
And tell me from
Africa up to this trimester"

Paranoid

At school my boys have learnt Auslan
Their hand signs I don't understand
I hear them giggle
And it's only a niggle
But I fear I'm the goal of their plan

Loves

8

I am sitting here with my lad
A moment shared just a tad
Then he turns to me
And he says with glee
You are the best mum I ever had

Absent

9

Calling my son for he is scant
"I know you can hear me" I rant
Silence echoes
Not even geckos
Then a little voice whispers "I can't"

Boundaries

Early morning, in bed and subdued
My son creeps in, slight intrude
I roll over to hug
He turns to me snug
And says "Personal space dude"

Villian

At the table where our dinner is set
My son talks of his day, he's upset
"The boy's a pig
a total prig
I tell you, he's a right Donald trumpet!"

Privacy

Time for Christmas wrapping, I get going
Boys try to find me, they're unknowing
"Don't come in" I say
"private stuff this way "
Boys ask through the door "what? Like
sewing?"

Attitude

In the shop, oh books hello!
Son wants to know if we can go
"Hey mum can you look
To see if there's a book
Called can we leave yet?" he bellows

Wisdom

Our son asks us what a super moon is
Dad answers this as he's the whiz
"A moon in the morning
Wears a cape without warning"
Son says "moons get up at night you diz"

Road Sign

15

Passing a road sign on a steep hill
"Sign says look out for elk, people"
"Mum, what are they?"
"Like deer in a way"
"No, I know that, but what are elk-people?"

Conspiracy

I'm helping my son alright
To find his choc from Santa's flight
But things are looking grim
Not sure how to tell him
I kind of ate it all last night

Compliment

Getting dressed with no fuss
My son walks in looking suss
"I see you are slightly fat"
He says to me, the little brat
"but to me mum, you'll always be flab-ulous!"

Evolution

18

Discussing evolution in the car,
"we came from monkeys, hey papa?"
Husband looks at me
Giggling with glee,
"Yes boys you certainly did", oh haha

Misunderstood

19

"Mum, how do you spell wiener?"
"to what is this that you refer?"
My youngest writes in
"the box they fight in"
"Oh", I say, "you mean arena!??"

Entrepreneur

"Mum I love you a bunch
And I will make your lunch"
"That would be great!
A sandwich lil' mate"
"Here Mum, that's a dollar thank you much"

Mother's Day

My son runs and hugs me to say
"You're nice on mother's day"
"You mean when you compare
"To the rest of the year?"
"Yes" he replies. Well okay

Milton Keynes UK
Ingram Content Group UK Ltd.
UKHW022203141023
430632UK00020B/674